LAUGH OUT LOUD!
THE HYSTERICAL HISTORY
JOKE BOOK

Sean Connolly

WINDMILL
BOOKS

New York

Published in 2013 by Windmill Books, An Imprint of Rosen Publishing
29 East 21st Street, New York, NY 10010

First Edition

Editor: Joe Harris
Illustrations: Adam Clay (cover) and Dynamo Design (interiors)
Layout Design: Notion Design

Library of Congress Cataloging-in-Publication Data

Connolly, Sean, 1956–
 The hysterical history joke book / by Sean Connolly. — 1st ed.
    p. cm. — (Laugh out loud)
 Includes index.
 ISBN 978-1-61533-645-6 (library binding) — ISBN 978-1-61533-656-2 (pbk.) —
 ISBN 978-1-61533-657-9 (6-pack)
 1. History—Juvenile humor. 2. Riddles, Juvenile. I. Title.
 PN6231.H47C55 2013
 808.88'2—dc23
                                                  2012019527

Printed in China

CPSIA Compliance Information: Batch #AW3102WM: For Further Information contact Windmill Books, New York, New York at 1-866-478-0556
SL002423US

CONTENTS

Jokes... 4

Glossary... 32

Index.. 32

Further Reading................................. 32

Websites... 32

When did early people start wearing uncreased clothes?
In the Iron Age!

What did Robin Hood wear to the Sherwood Forest ball?
A bow tie.

What was the moral of the story of Jonah and the whale?
You can't keep a good man down!

Teacher: Can you name a fierce warrior king?
Pupil: King Kong?

What sort of music did cavemen enjoy?
Rock music!

HYSTERICAL HISTORY

Teacher: Name an ancient musical instrument.
Pupil: An Anglo-saxophone?

What should you do if you see a caveman?
Go inside and explore, man!

What was Noah's job?
He was an ark-itect.

Why were undertakers in ancient Egypt such successful detectives?
They were good at wrapping up their cases.

What's purple and 5,000 miles long?
The grape wall of China.

Teacher: Surely you can remember what happened in 1776?
Pupil: It's all right for you—you were there!

Who was the fastest runner of all time?
Adam, because he was first in the human race!

Why did the king go to the dentist?
To get his teeth crowned.

Teacher: What were people wearing during the Great Fire of Chicago?
Pupil: Blazers, smoking jackets, and hose!

Why was England so wet in the nineteenth century?
Because Queen Victoria's reign lasted 64 years.

Which ancient leader invented seasonings?
Sultan Pepper!

Who succeeded the first President of the United States?
The second one.

Why did the very first fries not taste very nice?
Because they were fried in ancient Greece!

Teacher: Can you name a famous religious warrior?
Pupil: Attila the Nun!

Teacher: Where would you find a cowboy?
Pupil: In a field—and stop calling me "boy!"

What is an Egyptian mummy's favorite music?
Wrap music!

HYSTERICAL HISTORY

What do you call the Roman Emperor who kept pet mice?
Julius Cheeser!

How did Moses cut the sea in half?
With a sea-saw.

Teacher: How did knights make chain mail?
Pupil: From steel wool?

What's a buccaneer?
A good price for corn!

Where were French traitors beheaded?
Just above the shoulders!

Two wrongs don't make a right, but what do two rights make?
The first airplane!

Teacher: Why did Robin Hood steal from the rich?
Pupil: Because the poor didn't have anything worth stealing!

Teacher: How did the Dark Ages get their name?
Pupil: Because there were so many knights!

First Roman soldier: What's the time?
Second Roman soldier: XV past VIII.
First Roman soldier: By the time I work that out, it will be midnight!

What is an archaeologist?
Someone whose career is in ruins.

What do you call the king who invented the fireplace?
Alfred the Grate!

What did King Henry VIII do whenever he burped?
He issued a royal pardon.

Where was the Declaration of Independence signed?
At the bottom.

How did Vikings send secret messages?
By Norse code.

Which emperor should never have played with explosives?
Napoleon Blownapart!

Why do historians believe that Rome was built at night?
Because it wasn't built in a day.

In which battle was Alexander the Great killed?
His last one!

Why was George Washington buried at Mount Vernon?
Because he was dead.

What was King John's castle famous for?
Its knight life.

Which historical character was always eating?
Attila the Hungry!

What did Robin Hood say when he was almost hit at the archery tournament?
"That was an arrow escape!"

Teacher: Do you know the 42nd President of the United States?
Pupil: No, we've never been introduced.

What did Attila's wife say to get his attention?
"Over here, Hun."

What did King George think of the American colonists?
He thought that they were revolting.

HYSTERICAL HiSTORY

Why did King Arthur have a Round Table?
So that no one could corner him.

What do Alexander the Great and Billy the Kid have in common?
The same middle name.

How do we know that the ancient Romans had an expensive education?
Because they could all speak Latin.

Why couldn't the mummy answer the phone?
He was too wrapped up!

Who would referee a tennis match between Julius Caesar and Brutus?
A Roman umpire.

Why did Abraham Lincoln grow a beard?
He wanted to look like the guy on the five-dollar bill.

Did prehistoric people hunt bear?
No—they wore clothes!

When did the ancient Italians see most of the leaves falling from trees?
During the Fall of the Roman Empire.

What was written on the knight's tomb?
"May he rust in peace."

What was a caveman's favorite snack?
A club sandwich.

Which king had the largest crown?
The one with the biggest head!

Where did the Pilgrims land when they arrived in America?
On their feet.

In which era did people sunbathe the most?
The Bronzed Age.

What did the ancient Egyptians call bad leaders?
Un-Pharaohs.

What do Christopher Columbus, George Washington, and Martin Luther King, Jr. have in common?
They were all born on holidays.

Where do Egyptian mummies go for a swim?
To the Dead Sea.

Why does the Statue of Liberty stand in New York Harbor?
Because it can't sit down.

Why did Eve move to New York?
She fell for the Big Apple.

What do you call a blind dinosaur?
Doyouthinkhesaurus.

Why did the T. rex wear a Band-Aid?
He had a dino-sore!

What did General Patton do on Thanksgiving?
He gave tanks.

What would you get if you crossed the sixteenth president with a famous slugger?
Babe-raham Lincoln.

What do you call a pyramid overlooking the Nile?
A tomb with a view.

Which Italian explorer was best at aquatic sports?
Marco Water Polo.

Which Egyptian pharaoh played the trumpet?
Tootin' Kamun.

What do history teachers talk about when they get together?
The good old days.

What do you call a prehistoric monster when it is asleep?
A dino-snore.

Why did Columbus cross the ocean?
To get to the other tide.

Teacher: You know, an ancestor of mine came over on the Mayflower.
Pupil: Really? Which rat was he?

Which knight designed King Arthur's Round Table!
Sir Cumference!

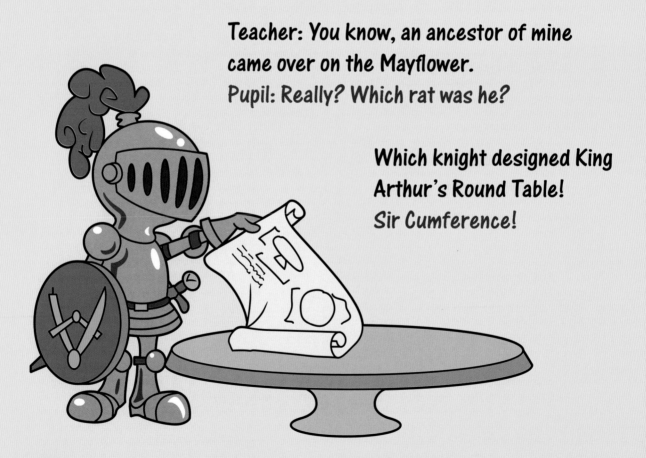

What was the first thing Queen Elizabeth I did when she ascended the throne?
She sat down.

Pupil: I wish I had been born 1,000 years ago.
Teacher: Why is that?
Pupil: Because I wouldn't have had to learn so much history!

How did the Roman cannibal feel about his mother-in-law?
Gladiator.

When does a baseball player wear armor?
In a knight game.

What happened when the wheel was invented?
It caused a revolution.

HYSTERICAL HISTORY

Did Adam and Eve ever have a date?
No, but they had an apple!

What did George Washington feed his cattle?
Fodder of our country.

How was the Roman Empire cut in half?
With a pair of Caesars.

Where did Napoleon keep his armies?
Up his sleevies.

Why did the court jester swallow fire?
Because he wanted to burn some calories.

What happened when electricity was discovered?
Someone got a nasty shock.

Why did the nervous knight withdraw from the archery contest?
It was an arrowing experience.

How did Robin Hood tie his bootlaces?
With a long bow.

What did Thomas Edison's mother say when he showed her the electric light he had invented?
"That's wonderful, dear. Now turn it off and go to bed."

Why did the Romans build straight roads?
So the soldiers didn't go around the bend.

Why did the mammoth have a woolly coat? Because it would have looked silly in a parka.

Why were Pilgrims' pants always falling down?
Because they wore their belts around their hats.

Teacher: What came after the Stone Age and the Bronze Age?
Pupil: The sausage?

What did the witch say to Paul Bunyan at the edge of the forest?
I wooden go there.

What is the difference between a duck and George Washington?
One has a bill on his face and the other has his face on a bill.

What happened to the knight who lost his left arm and left leg in battle?
He was all right in the end.

What did the turkey say to the Pilgrim holding a musket?
"Look over there—it's a deer!"

Which historical figure entered the Olympic swimming event without a bathing suit?
Lady Good-diver.

How did Columbus's men sleep on the boat?
With their eyes shut.

Why did King Arthur build Camelot?
So he could park his camels.

What did Mount Vesuvius say to Pompeii?
I lava you.

What do you call an archaeologist that sleeps all the time?
Lazy bones.

Which protest by a group of cats and dogs took place in 1773?
The Boston Flea Party.

Why did Captain Cook sail to Australia?
It was too far to swim.

What did Columbus do after he crossed the Atlantic?
He dried his clothes.

Why did Cleopatra take milk baths? She couldn't find a cow tall enough for her to take a shower.

Why does it take pirates a long time to learn the alphabet? Because they spend so long at "C."

Which Viking explorer had a greenhouse on his longboat? Leaf Eriksson.

What do you call George Washington's false teeth? Presi-dentures.

Why did the knight always carry a can opener? In case a bee flew into his armor.

Why did the pioneers cross America in covered wagons? Because they didn't want to wait thirty years for the first train.

Why was Charlemagne able to draw such straight lines?
He was a good ruler.

What did Noah use to find his way in the dark?
Floodlights.

What king invented fractions?
King Henry the $\frac{1}{8}$th.

Why were the first European settlers in America like ants?
Because they lived in colonies.

Teacher: Can anyone tell me where Hadrian's Wall is?
Pupil: I think it's around Hadrian's backyard.

What has two eyes, two legs, and two noses?
Two pirates.

What did they call the cartoonists in Washington's Continental Army?
Yankee doodlers.

Why did the mammoth have a trunk?
Because it would have looked silly with suitcases.

Which Native American tribe has always had the most lawyers?
The Sioux.

Where was the Ink-an Empire?
In Pen-sylvania.

What did the executioner say to the former king?
It's time to head off!

What did the cowboy say when he saw a cow in a tree?
Howdy get there?

Which of Queen Elizabeth's explorers tried to ride a bike from England to America?
Sir Walter Raleigh.

Which pirate told the most jokes?
Captain Kidd.

What did the patriots wear to the Boston Tea Party?
T-shirts.

Why did George Washington have trouble sleeping?
Because he couldn't lie.

Who made dinner for Robin Hood and his Merry Men?
Frier Tuck.

If you cloned Henry IV, what would you get?
Henry IV, Part II.

What was the most popular movie in ancient Greece?
Troy Story.

Glossary

archaeologist (ahr-kee-AH-luh-jist) someone who digs up objects from the ground and uses them to study the past

ascend (uh-SEND) to climb up

buccaneer (buh-kuh-NEER) a daring pirate

colonist (KAH-luh-nist) someone who settles in an area under the control of another country

Confederate (kun-FEH-duh-ret) a supporter of the Southern states in the Civil War

sultan (SUL-tin) a Muslim ruler from the Middle East

tournament (TOR-nuh-ment) a medieval jousting competition

Further Reading

Deary, Terry. *Awful Egyptians.* Horrible Histories. New York: Scholastic, 2009.

Time for Kids. *Presidents of the United States.* New York: Collins, 2007.

Lichtenheld, Tom. *Everything I Know About Pirates.* New York: Simon and Schuster Books for Young Readers, 2003.

Index

Attila the Hun 7, 12

Egypt, ancient 5, 7, 15, 16, 17

Greece, ancient 7, 31

Hood, Robin 4, 9, 12, 23, 31

Kings 4, 6, 10, 11, 12, 13, 15, 18, 25, 28, 30, 31

Knights 8, 9, 11, 14, 18, 19, 23, 25, 27

Pilgrims 15, 18, 21, 24, 25

pirates 8, 20, 27, 29, 30

presidents 7, 11, 12, 14, 15, 17, 24, 27, 29, 31

queens 6, 19, 27, 30

Romans 8, 9, 11, 13, 14, 19, 21, 22, 23

Vikings 10, 21, 27

Websites

For Web resources related to the subject of this book, go to: www.windmillbooks.com/weblinks and select this book's title.